Pinball to Gaming Systems $19.95

Discover how the pinball machine evolved into the massively multiplayer online gaming systems we have today.

#2113042   J. Colby   Available:08/01/2019   24 pgs
Grade:234   Dewey:608   LEX:810

Printing Press to 3D Printing $19.95

Discover how the printing press evolved into the 3D printing technology we have today.

#2113043   J. Colby   Available:08/01/2019   24 pgs
Grade:234   Dewey:608   LEX:820

Silent Films to 3D Movies $19.95

Discover how silent films evolved into the cinema we have today.

#2113044   J. Colby   Available:08/01/2019   24 pgs
Grade:234   Dewey:608   LEX:740

Telephone to Smartphones $19.95

Discover how the first telephone evolved into the smartphones we have today.

#2113045   J. Colby   Available:08/01/2019   24 pgs
Grade:234   Dewey:608   LEX:770

Printing Press to 3D Printing
Then to Now Tech

By Jennifer Colby

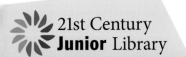

21st Century
Junior Library

Published in the United States of America by
Cherry Lake Publishing
Ann Arbor, Michigan
www.cherrylakepublishing.com

Content Adviser: Adam Fulton Johnson, PhD History of Science and Technology, University of Michigan
Reading Adviser: Marla Conn, MS, Ed., Literacy specialist, Read-Ability, Inc.

Photo Credits: ©klom/Shutterstock.com, Cover, 1 [left]; ©science photo/Shutterstock.com, Cover, 2 [right];
©Victor Wong/Shutterstock.com, 4; ©Everett Historical/Shutterstock.com, 6; ©Stavchansky Yakov/Shutterstock.com, 8;
©RossEdwardCairney/Shutterstock.com, 10; ©giocalde/Shutterstock.com, 12; ©KOKTARO/Shutterstock.com, 14;
©FabrikaSimf/Shutterstock.com, 16; ©guteksk7/Shutterstock.com, 18; ©Kyrylo Gilvin/Shutterstock.com, 20

Library of Congress Cataloging-in-Publication Data has been filed and is available at catalog.loc.gov

Cherry Lake Publishing would like to acknowledge the work of the Partnership for 21st Century Skills.
Please visit *www.p21.org* for more information.

Printed in the United States of America
Corporate Graphics

CONTENTS

In China, wood blocks were used to handprint books. Designs were cut into pieces of wood that were then used for printing.

Printing for the Masses

Johannes Gutenberg created his printing press in Germany in the 15th century. Printing presses allow books to be printed by machine instead of being copied by hand. But mass printing **techniques** were used as early as the 7th century in China.

Here is a painting of Gutenberg's printing press.

A Better Press

Others had created **mechanical** printing presses before Gutenberg's. But Gutenberg used a better mix of metals to create movable **type**. He also introduced oil-based ink. And he used nicer paper. All of his **improvements** made his press more popular.

Writing books by hand was a slow process.

Before the **invention** of the printing press, **scribes** copied books and **documents** by hand. These books were expensive!

Look!

What were other early printing inventions? Ask an adult to help you look on the internet to find some.

New letter styles were created by printers.

Changes over Time

With the invention of the printing press, books could be printed more cheaply. Publishers created presses that could print smaller books. These more **portable** books were very popular.

Printers began making more improvements to their presses. New **fonts** were developed. **Plates** using different color inks were used. A Dutch printer

Full-color ads became popular in magazines.

invented a press in the 17th century that could make copies of old books. It was the first copy machine!

New developments in the 18th century allowed for mass printing of magazines. Full-color printing became popular in the early 1800s. Ads and postcards were printed for public use everywhere.

New printing techniques in the 20th century resulted in many of the products we make today. Do you have a T-shirt with an image or words on it? You can thank Englishman Samuel Simon for patenting the screen printing technique in 1907.

T-shirts are usually screen printed.

In screen printing, ink is pressed through a mesh screen with a **squeegee**. The pattern in the screen lets colors transfer to cloth or paper in a specific design pattern.

Ask Questions!

What other printed products have been around since the early 20th century? Ask an adult about items from an **offset printer**, like greeting cards, paperback books, newspapers, and magazines.

Laser printers create static electricity to transfer powdered ink to a surface.

Digital Heads into the Future

New printing techniques in the late 20th century involved computers. Digital printers make it possible for anyone to create professional-looking documents. Images or words are created on a computer and transferred into digital files that are printed with **toner** or ink onto many types of materials.

Have you seen a 3D printer in action? They have become more popular now than when they were first invented in the 1980s.

Laser printers were invented in 1975. Some were as big as a car! Today, these digital printers are much smaller. It is very common for people to have an inkjet printer or a laser printer in their home.

For a long time, most printing methods were flat or 2D. But in 1981, Japanese researcher Hideo Kodama invented the first version of a 3D printer.

Think!

How do you think 3D printers work? What types of materials do they use to print with? Ask an adult to help you search the internet.

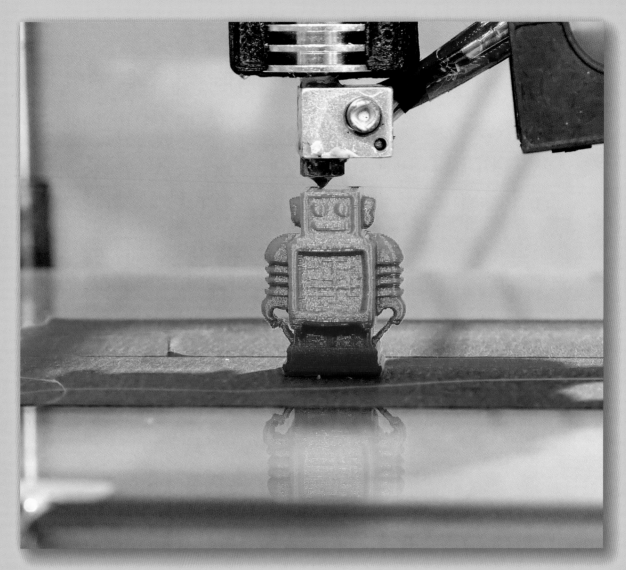

3D printers use many types of materials.

A 3D printer creates an object by adding one layer of material at a time. A digital model is created using computer-aided drafting software. The digital model is split into layers. Each layer is a **blueprint**. The blueprint files tell the printer how to create the object.

Today, 3D printers can print with metal, ceramics, chocolate, and more. The possibilities of 3D printing are endless!

Make a Guess!

What changes do you think there will be in printing? Talk about it with friends and make a list.

GLOSSARY

blueprint (BLOO-print) a detailed plan of how to make something

documents (DAHK-yuh-muhnts) important papers that give information about something

fonts (FAHNTS) sets of letters, numbers, and punctuation marks that are all one size and style

improvements (im-PROOV-muhnts) additions or changes that make something better

invention (in-VEN-shun) something useful that is created for the first time

mechanical (muh-KAN-ih-kuhl) relating to machines

offset printer (AWF-set PRINT-ur) a printing technique where an inked image is transferred from a plate to a rubber blanket and then to the printing surface

plates (PLAYTS) metal surfaces that different color inks are applied to

portable (POR-tuh-buhl) easy to carry or move around

scribes (SKRIBES) people who copy documents by hand

squeegee (SKWEE-jee) a tool with a rubber blade attached to a handle that is used for spreading liquid across a print screen

techniques (tek-NEEKS) ways of doing something

toner (TOH-nur) powdered ink used in laser printing

type (TIPE) printed letters

FIND OUT MORE

BOOKS

Abell, Tracy. *3D Printing*. Calgary, Canada: Weigl Publishers, 2018.

Sabelko, Rebecca. *The Printing Press*. Minnetonka, MN: Bellwether Media, 2019.

WEBSITES

3D Hubs—What Is 3D Printing?
https://www.3dhubs.com/what-is-3d-printing
Learn how 3D printing works.

iKids—Invention Ideas: Where Do They Come From?
http://inventivekids.com/invention-ideas
Learn about the different types of invention inspirations.

INDEX

ABOUT THE AUTHOR

Jennifer Colby is a school librarian in Ann Arbor, Michigan. She loves reading, traveling, and going to museums to learn about new things.